The Art of War

The Art of War

A Treatise on Chinese Military Science
Compiled about 500 B.C.

HEIAN INTERNATIONAL, INC.

©1982 Graham Brash, Ltd.
First published by Graham Brash, Ltd. Singapore

First American Edition 1999
99 00 01 02 03 04 05 10 9 8 7 6 5 4 3 2 1

HEIAN INTERNATIONAL, INC.
1815 West 205th Street, Suite #301
Torrance, CA 90501

Web Site: www.heian.com
E-mail: heianemail@heian.com

ISBN: 0-89346-921-1

Printed in Singapore

Contents

Introduction

The origins and authorship of China's oldest military classic, *The Art of War*, remain unknown, but it is generally believed that the book in its present form is a composite of several military treatises which existed during the period of the Warring States (476–221 B.C.). Hence a certain amount of repetition and disjointed thoughts which we have tried to minimise in this translation, e.g. chapter 11, and a few irrelevant introductory remarks which we have omitted, e.g. chapters 7 and 8.

Much literature on military science was either lost or destroyed as Confucianism gained ascendancy in China and pacifism supplanted militancy. *The Art of War* remained in obscurity until Emperor Wu, a great soldier and statesman of the Wei Dynasty (55–220 A.D.), produced a new edition with a personal commentary. Since then there have been many other annotated Chinese editions. The first translation was by a Jesuit priest in 1772 (*Art Militaire des Chinois*) and the first English translation appeared in 1910.

Over 2000 years have passed since the original book was compiled, yet *The Art of War* remains surprisingly full of sound, relevant thinking and instruction on traditional combat and warfare.

1

Planning

War determines life and death, the rise and fall of a State. It is therefore of vital importance that the art of war should be studied with great care.

In the study of warfare these five principles should be considered:

(1) The Moral Cause. A just and noble cause will unite the men with their leader. They will follow him through every vicissitude and gladly sacrifice their lives.

(2) The Climate. Consideration must be given to the weather, the seasons and the time of day or night.

(3) The Terrain. Similarly, careful account must be taken of the nature of the land, distances to be covered and difficulties likely to be encountered on the way.

(4) The Command. The general must be an outstanding leader — wise, loyal to his men, brave, compassionate yet firm.

(5) Organisation and Discipline. Order and the

skilful management of men and affairs are essential, so that every advantage may be fully utilised.

The general who thoroughly understands and applies these five principles will be victorious. If he ignores them, he will be defeated.

Based on the answers to the following questions, the outcome of a war can be forecast:

(1) Which party has the stronger moral cause?

(2) Which has the better general?

(3) Which has the advantage of climate and terrain?

(4) Which has the superior army — better trained officers, more disciplined men, order and efficient management, a better system of rewards and punishments?

The generals who can deliberate in this fashion will surely win and their services must be retained. The generals who do not consider these questions are bound to lose and should be dismissed.

A good general should be able to deal with all kinds of emergencies and modify his plans to suit changing circumstances in order to achieve the best results.

War is mainly a game of deception. The strong should

feign weakness, the active inactivity. If the goal is near, pretend it is far away. If the objective is far off, pretend that it is close.

Lull the enemy with small "victories"; entice them with bait. Then attack and throw them into complete disorder so that they may be crushed with ease.

If the enemy are powerful, extra care must be taken in one's preparations. Know and avoid the enemy's strong points, attack their weaknesses. If they are angry, provoke them further. Pretend to be weak to make them arrogant and over-confident. When they are eager for action, weary them with delays. When they are united, try to create discord and internal dissension. Attack where and when least expected.

All these considerations, which are essential to military success, must be kept secret.

From the way a war is planned, one can forecast its outcome. Careful planning will lead to success and careless planning to defeat. How much more certain is defeat if there is no planning at all!

2

Preparations

In the conduct of a war thousands of chariots and carriages and tens of thousands of soldiers may be deployed. Provisions may have to be transported over thousands of *li* (a Chinese mile). The total expenses for an army of one hundred thousand may amount to thousands of *taels* of silver per day.

When victory is long delayed the enthusiasm of the army may be diminished. A long siege exhausts the men. A protracted war impoverishes the Treasury. When thus over-extended, a country offers a golden opportunity to its other enemies and, in its weakened condition, even its most resourceful leaders will be of no avail.

The foolish may sometimes win a quick victory, but even the cleverest men will fail in a protracted war. Prolonged fighting has never benefited any country, vanquished or victorious.

Those who are not fully aware of the dangers of war cannot wage war profitably.

The experienced leader will ensure that there does not have to be a second conscription of men and that provisions do not have to be replenished more than twice. Supplied with adequate arms, the army should be made to live by foraging on the enemy. In this way there will be adequate food for the men.

Military provisions transported long distances would impoverish the government as well as the populace.

War causes inflation which in turn depletes resources. As a country becomes poorer, levies and taxes become heavier. People may lose as much as seven-tenths of their possessions and the State use up as much as three-fifths of its total revenue. Therefore a wise general makes it possible for the army to live off the enemy. A small amount of food seized from the enemy is worth twenty times one's own.

Men are incited to kill by provocation and enticed to win by loot.

The first to capture ten chariots or more should be rewarded, and, after changing colours, the captured chariots should be put to use, while the prisoners should be treated kindly. The way to increase one's own strength is by appropriating the resources of the vanquished.

To sum up, one should aim at a swift victory and avoid protracted wars.

The experienced in warfare control the welfare of the people and the safety of the State.

3

Strategy

It is better to subdue than to destroy an enemy State, army, regiment, company, even squadron.

To conquer the enemy without having to resort to war is a greater achievement than fighting to win every battle.

The highest form of military leadership is to overcome the enemy by strategy. The next best way is to absorb the enemy through an alliance. Third best is to conquer the enemy in battle. The least satisfactory means of victory is to lay siege to walled cities.

This should be avoided if at all possible, for it takes at least three months to make all the preparations, and another three months to build the siege ladders. Impatience might lead to reckless, futile attacks resulting in the loss of many men. Such are the dangers of laying siege to a walled city.

Through clever strategy skilful leaders can conquer the enemy without fighting battles, capture cities without laying siege to them and annex States without prolonged warfare. They can control an Empire without endangering their men, or win a complete victory without even wearying them.

If you outnumber the enemy by ten to one, surround them; by five to one, attack them; by two to one, divide them. If you are equally matched, take the offensive. If the enemy forces are slightly stronger, prepare for defence; if vastly superior, retreat, for no matter how valiantly a small force may fight, it must succumb in the end to greater strength and numbers.

Generals are guardians of the State. Their proficiency in warfare is the country's strength, their deficiency its weakness.

A sovereign may bring disaster on his army if:

(1) he interferes in military command and orders an advance or a retreat at the wrong time,

(2) he causes disorder in the army by making the mistake of treating military matters in the same way as civil matters, and

(3) he undermines the morale of officers and men by appointing commanders who are ignorant and inept.

Bringing disorder into the army is tantamount to

inviting defeat by the enemy who are sure to take advantage of a demoralised army.

The five ways to victory are:

(1) to know when to fight and when not to fight,

(2) to know how to match a small force against a large one,

(3) to have the whole-hearted support of all the men,

(4) to seize every possible advantage or opportunity, and

(5) to be able to lead and command without interference from the sovereign.

In conclusion, it may be said that the leader who has a thorough knowledge of his own as well as enemy conditions is sure to win. The man who knows his own condition but not the enemy's has an even chance of victory. But the man who has no knowledge of either his own or enemy conditions is bound to lose every battle.

4

Tactics

In ancient times great military leaders would first ensure their own invulnerability, then wait for an opportunity to defeat the enemy. Security against defeat depends on one's own efforts, whereas the opportunity of victory depends partly on the enemy. Thus, even the greatest leaders can only secure themselves against defeat. They cannot be sure of an opportunity for victory. It may be said that no one can be absolutely sure of victory.

Securing against defeat requires defensive tactics, fighting for victory requires offensive tactics. With an inferior force, defence is the more advisable course; with a superior force, it is better to attack.

A leader experienced in defensive tactics is able to position his forces in safe, inaccessible places. A general adept in offensive tactics is able to position his troops at all vantage points. The one aims to keep his forces intact, the other to crush the enemy.

Lifting a strand of hair does not indicate unusual strength, being able to see the sun and the moon does not indicate sharp vision, being able to hear thunder does not indicate sensitive hearing. Similarly, a victory which anyone could win or the conquest of an empire by mass slaughter does not merit the highest praise.

According to the ancients, the truly great in warfare are those who not only win but win with such ease and ingenuity that their wisdom and courage often go unrecognised. Such men do their best to ensure that victory will be theirs before they even commence fighting, placing themselves in an invulnerable position and not missing any opportunity to defeat the enemy. The winner does everything to ensure success before he fights. The loser rushes into combat without adequate preparation.

To be sure of victory the wise in warfare see to it that they first have a strong moral cause and that the army is well disciplined.

The science of war may be summarised under these headings:

(1) Measurement of distances

(2) Estimation of expenses

(3) Evaluation of forces

(4) Assessment of possibilities

(5) Planning for victory.

Having measured geographical distances, we make an estimate of expenses. Based on the estimation of expenses, we evaluate the strength of the forces. On the strength of the forces, we assess the possibilities of success and failure. On our assessment of the possibilities, we plan for victory.

A confident army easily outmatches a fearful army, just as twenty *taels* outweigh one-twenty fourth of a *tael*. A confident army attacking is like flood waters pouring into a chasm thousands of fathoms deep.

5

Organisation

Controlling a large army is the same as controlling a small army. It is only a matter of organisation. Similarly, whether fighting against a large or small army, one should follow the same guiding principles of good organisation and efficient communication.

Soldiers should be carefully divided into regulars and reserves so that the attacks of the enemy may be successfully repulsed.

An attack should have the forceful impact of a grindstone crushing eggs. To do this the strength and weaknesses of the enemy must first be ascertained.

In battle the regulars should be used first. Reserves should be used with care. Marshalling reserves requires the resourcefulness of sky, land and sea; the versatility of the sun and moon; the continuity of the four seasons.

Various combinations of just five musical notes can produce endless melodies. Combinations of just five colours can create boundless beauty. Combinations of just five flavours can produce an unlimited variety of delicious food. Similarly, when attacking, one is restricted to using either regulars or reserves, but the variation is infinite. Who can know all the possible variations? One method may lead to another, like moving in a circle and never reaching the end.

With sudden force rushing torrents move boulders. With correct timing the hovering falcon pounces on its prey. In like manner the skilful leader attacks with terrifying speed and perfect timing. On the verge of attack his army is like a taut bow, in attacking like a trigger released.

Troop movements may appear confused and disorderly, but in reality everything is done according to plan and order.

To simulate disorder there must be strict discipline. To simulate fear requires great courage. To simulate weakness one must be strong.

Order or disorder depends on organisation. Courage or fear depends on how an attack is implemented. Strength or weakness depends on appearances.

Weary the enemy by making them chase after false prizes. Entice them from their secure position and then ambush them.

The skilful general seeks victory from an opportune situation, relying less on the efforts of individuals. He selects the men to suit the situation (just as a builder selects the right materials for the job). Logs and stones placed on a firm base remain stable. When they are placed on an insecure foundation they tend to shift. In a corner they remain still. Remember, the nature of a round object is to roll.

A great general pushes his army forward just as gravity and momentum create an avalanche thousands of feet down a mountain slope.

6

Seizing Opportunities

The army which reaches the battlefield early has time to rest while waiting for the enemy. The army which reaches the battlefield late has to rush into action while still weary and exhausted.

The skilful general makes the enemy traverse great distances and encounter many dangers to meet him, while he waits at ease. He entices the enemy into going where he wishes them to be and prevents them from reaching their objective. He will not let them rest when weary or eat though food is plentiful. He forces them to move on when they wish to make camp.

Attack where enemy forces are expected to appear, appear where they do not expect an attack.

If an army can travel thousands of *li* without feeling weary, it must be due to the absence of opposition.

Attack where the enemy's defence is weak. Defend from an impregnable position. In attacking, do not let the enemy find a strong position of defence. In defending, leave the enemy at a loss at to where to attack.

Be subtle, unpredictable, almost mystical, intangible! In this way you will control the fate of the enemy.

If you direct your attacks against the enemy's weak points, your advance becomes irresistible.

When an army can travel faster than the enemy it can retreat without danger of pursuit and capture.

If you wish to draw the enemy out of an inaccessible stronghold, attack some other position which they have to defend. If you do not wish to engage in battle and would rather remain fixed in your position, mislead the enemy with unexpected sorties.

If you know the battle plans of the enemy and at the same time can keep them ignorant of yours, you can concentrate your forces and divide theirs, so that your whole army can be pitted against their disintegrated groups.

Do not reveal where you plan to attack, so that the enemy will have to prepare to defend several possible places, thereby further scattering their forces and weakening their resistance at any one point. If they concentrate on defending their rear, their front line will be weak; if they concentrate in front, their rear will be vulnerable to attack. If they strengthen the defence of their right flank, the left will be weak; and if they strengthen the left, the right will suffer. If they spread their forces in all directions, their defence will be weak all round.

The defending army generally finds that its forces are inadequate, whereas the army on the attack finds its forces more than adequate.

If you cannot anticipate the time and place of a coming battle, you cannot coordinate your forces although they are nearby — not to mention those which are many *li* away.

It may be said that victory depends on accurate anticipation of enemy movements. Failure to do this could lead to the defeat of even a superior force.

Though the enemy are strong they can be rendered impotent. Through spies one can ascertain their plans and plots; through provocation their mood and movements; by tactics their strength and weakness; and by contact the differences between the two opposing forces.

The consummate tactician is able to conceal his plans so that even the cleverest spies cannot detect anything and even the most skilful commanders cannot formulate counter plans.

To vanquish a superior force by clever tactics is beyond the comprehension of the masses. They see the victory but cannot understand the tactics which achieved it.

Tactics should not be repeated in ensuing battles, but varied continually according to the circumstances.

The guiding principle in military tactics may be compared to the nature of water. Just as water flows from a higher level to a lower level, an army should avoid strength and attack weakness. Just as water adapts to the contours of the land, an army should adapt its plans to suit the enemy. Just as water has no fixed form, warfare has no inflexible rules.

Those who are able to vary military tactics according to the nature of the enemy may be compared to gods. They are as versatile as the five elements, the four seasons, the sun and the moon which wax and wane forever.

7

Manoeuvres

Manoeuvres may be difficult to understand because the direct often seems devious and the advantageous disadvantageous.

Entice the enemy into taking a roundabout route, so that you may arrive first at the battle-ground even though you set off late.

It is a great advantage to be able to outwit the enemy by clever manoeuvring, for it is dangerous to have to face their full combat strength.

To transport all the necessary equipment may retard your advance, but to leave equipment behind may result in the serious loss of supplies.

Consequently, if a leader tries to win some advantageous position by forcing his men to abandon their equipment and march hurriedly day and night over one hundred *li*, he may end up by being utterly defeated and losing his commanders. Only the strongest men will arrive on time, the weary lagging behind, so that not more than one in ten men will be in battle position.

If a forced march covers fifty *li*, not more than half the men will arrive on time, and the vanguard is likely to be defeated.

If the march covers even thirty *li*, not more than two-thirds of the men are likely to be in position on time.

An army which loses its baggage, provisions or supply base will surely perish.

A State sovereign should not enter into an alliance with other sovereigns before he is well acquainted with their plans.

Do not conduct a war before studying the layout of the land — its mountains, forests, passes, lakes, rivers, etc.

Employ skilful guides to make full use of all natural advantages.

War is motivated by gain and based on deception. Its tactics lie in varying the deployment of your forces.

You must be able to move like the wind or stand firm as a forest; be as destructive as fire or as unmoveable as a mountain; remain as impenetrable as darkness or strike suddenly like a thunderbolt.

When clearing the countryside the soldiers should be dispersed in all directions. When occupying a country they should be distributed to hold key points.

Weigh all possibilities before making a move, acquire the art of being devious before hoping to win. This is an important point in military manoeuvres.

An ancient treatise on military science states, "When words cannot be heard, signal with gongs and drums. When eyes cannot see clearly in the distance, signal with banners and flags." By such signals control and direct the men so that they act as one, with neither the bravest advancing on his own nor the most cowardly retreating on his own. Signal with fires and drums by night, with banners and flags by day, thereby controlling troop movements at all times.

An entire army may become demoralised, just as a general may grow discouraged.

In the early stages of battle the fighting spirit is strong, but later it tends to flag. Towards the end it may die out altogether. So the wise general tries to avoid encounters with the enemy when their spirits are high and to attack when their spirits are low. He understands and makes use of these emotional states.

His troops are orderly, in contrast with the enemy's disorder; his men are calm while the enemy's are anxious and fearful. He is in control of their mental states.

He remains close when the enemy would be distant, rests when they toil, feasts while they starve. He is master of their physical states.

Do not attack when enemy banners indicate that their troops are in good order and condition. Do not give chase when their movements show that they are well organised. Vary your plans according to the circumstances.

Do not attack uphill or confront the enemy with your back against a mountain. Do not pursue if they merely simulate flight. Do not challenge them when their fighting spirit is strong. Do not be tempted by false "bait". Do not stop the enemy if they are determined to return home. When laying siege, leave them a way of retreat. Do not drive a defeated enemy to desperation.

These are guiding points in the conduct of war.

8

Variation in Tactics

Sometimes there are roads which must not be taken, forces which must not be attacked, cities which should not be besieged, positions which should not be contested and commands of sovereigns best disobeyed.

The general who understands the advantages of varying his tactics really knows the art of war.

The general who does not appreciate the need to vary his tactics cannot turn natural advantages to account, although he may be familiar with the layout of the land. The general who appreciates the need but does not know how to vary his tactics cannot make the best use of his men.

The wise man considers both favourable and unfavourable factors, the former to pursue his objectives and the latter to extricate himself from difficulties.

Kingdoms can be cowered by the infliction of heavy damage, wearied by constant harassment and lured by temptation of gain.

Do not rely on the enemy's failure to come, but prepare instead how to confront them successfully; do not rely on the enemy's failure to attack, but consider instead how to make your own position unassailable.

A general may be at fault in five different ways:

(1) If he is reckless, he is easily killed.

(2) If he is afraid of dying, he is easily captured.

(3) If quick tempered, he is easily provoked.

(4) If too sensitive about his honour, he is easily insulted.

(5) If over concerned about his men, he is easily harassed.

These five common weaknesses can prove disastrous in warfare. When an army suffers a crushing defeat or a general is slain, the cause can often be traced to one of these weaknesses which should, therefore, be clearly understood and avoided.

9

Sites and Observations

This chapter deals with encamping the army and observing the enemy.

If possible, avoid mountains and keep to the valleys, but, if engaged in mountain warfare, stay on high ground and fight downhill, not uphill.

Similarly, in river combat, keep to high ground and fight downstream, not upsteam. If you wish to make a stand after crossing a river, choose a position some distance from it. If you plan to attack at a river, conceal your forces on the river bank and intercept the enemy in midstream or ambush them when they are about to land.

Do not linger on marshy terrain. If forced to fight in a marsh, stay where there are reeds, and trees to the rear.

In open country encamp on high ground with your right flank and your rear well protected, so that only the front is open to attack. Make sure that you have a means of safe retreat at your rear.

Because he was experienced in these four kinds of warfare, Emperor Huang was able to defeat other feudal lords.

Take care over the daily diet and living quarters of the troops so that they may be healthy and therefore more likely to win.

All armies prefer high to low ground, sunshine to shade. When camping on a hill, occupy the sunny side and face downhill. Make use of such natural advantages.

When it is necessary to ford a river during heavy rain, wait till the water begins to subside.

Avoid country with precipitous cliffs, deep caverns, inaccessible recesses, tangled undergrowth, treacherous quagmires or dangerous crevasses. When the terrain is difficult, face it and let it be to the rear of the enemy. Drive them towards it.

When an army finds itself in the neighbourhood of dangerous passes, ponds filled with reeds or woods with thick undergrowth, a most careful and thorough search is necessary for these places provide excellent cover for the enemy.

If the enemy appear undisturbed when approached, it

indicates that they are confident of their safety.

When the enemy come out a long way to make a challenge, it indicates that they are anxious for the other party to approach.

When the enemy occupy a seemingly vulnerable position, they may be setting a trap.

Motion in a forest indicates that the enemy are approaching.

Grassland bestrewn with obstacles may indicate that the enemy intend to lead you astray.

Birds suddenly taking flight or animals startled out of their haunts indicate an enemy ambush.

High clouds of dust indicate the approach of chariots.

Clouds of dust, more low lying but over a larger area, indicate the approach of infantry.

Clouds of dust in different directions indicate that the enemy are collecting firewood.

When clouds of dust are few and scattered, the enemy are encamping.

When the speech of their messengers is humble, but at the same time the enemy are increasingly preparing for war, it means that they are about to attack.

When the speech of their messengers is arrogant, but at the same time enemy movements appear nervous and hasty, it means that they are about to retreat.

When light chariots advance along the flanks, it may be assumed that the enemy are in battle formation, ready for combat.

If the enemy suddenly sue for peace when there is no cause, beware of a trick.

When there is unusual and prolonged activity in the enemy camp, they are preparing for action and are about to attack.

When the enemy advance and retreat half-heartedly, they are probably trying to draw you forwards.

When men are seen leaning (wearily) on their arms and equipment, food is probably scarce.

When water carriers have to rush around to quench the men's thirst, there is a scarcity of water.

When the enemy fail to seize an obvious advantage, it

is a sign of their weariness.

Where birds are seen in great numbers, it may be assumed that the place is empty of men.

Crying during the night indicates fear.

Frequent disorder and dissension among the troops indicate a lack of strong authority.

A constant shifting of banners and flags suggests the possibility of a rebellion.

When officers lose their tempers easily with their men, it means that they are weary of war.

When horses are feasted with grain and men with meat, when cooking vessels are destroyed and the troops abandon their camp, it is clear that they are determined to pursue their enemy to the limit.

Constant whispering and murmuring among the men indicate a general dissatisfaction in the army.

If the commanding officer has to resort to offering rewards and bribes to push his men on, the army must be near the end of its tether.

If the commanding officer has to resort frequently to

punishment, his army is in dire distress.

If he has to act without consistency, first bullying and then entreating his men, it is evident that his army greatly lacks order and discipline.

When the enemy send envoys with lavish compliments, it indicates that they desire peace.

When the enemy appear greatly provoked and yet do nothing, neither attacking nor retreating, great caution and vigilance need to be exercised.

The strength of an army does not lie in mere numbers. Advance does not depend on valour alone. The general who is able to use all available forces to best advantage and to anticipate enemy moves correctly will surely be successful.

He who fails to plan ahead and also underestimates the enemy is sure to be defeated.

When men are ruled by punishment instead of affection and respect for their superiors, they will not obey whole-heartedly and cannot be trusted. On the other hand, men who do have affection and regard for their leader but who nevertheless will not accept discipline cannot be trusted either.

An army which is amenable to kind treatment as well as discipline will be invincible.

Discipline must be enforced with fairness and consistency to win the complete support and obedience of the troops.

A leader who commands the obedience and confidence of his men can make them do almost anything he wishes, for the common good.

10

Terrain

Generally, there are the following types of terrain:

(1) Accessible

(2) Difficult

(3) Indifferent

(4) Restricted

(5) Precipitous

(6) Extensive.

Accessible Terrain affords free and easy access to both combatants, so that he who first occupies the high sunny ground and protects his supply route has the advantage.

Difficult Terrain makes exit easier than entry. On this type of ground, surprise is an important factor. The enemy can be defeated if caught unprepared. However, if you are not successful at the first attempt, it might be difficult, even disastrous, to try a second attack.

Indifferent Terrain makes it disadvantageous for either party to make the first move. On this kind of ground, do not be lured forwards. Instead, pretend to retreat and then attack the enemy when they have left their position. In this way victory might be possible.

On Restricted Terrain with mountainous slopes and narrow passes, try to be the first to occupy the passes which should then be strongly guarded against the approach of the enemy. Should the enemy reach the passes first, attack or retreat will depend on how strongly they are guarded.

On Precipitous or Mountainous Terrain try to be the first to occupy the sunny side of the steep hills or mountains, there to await the enemy. If the enemy should be there first, do not pursue them but try instead to entice them into leaving their position.

On Extensive Terrain the chances of the two parties are even, and it is difficult, even disadvantageous, for either side to attack first.

The above principles regarding the six types of terrain and how leaders should deploy their troops in each circumstance should be clearly understood.

An army may be destroyed by:

(1) Flight

(2) Insubordination

(3) Collapse

(4) Ruin

(5) Disorganisation

(6) Rout.

These six calamities are not due to natural causes but to the fault of the generals.

Other conditions being equal, a concentrated force will put to Flight a divided force.

Insubordination results from strong men having weak officers.

However, strong officers leading weak men will result in the Collapse of an army.

If officers are resentful and disobedient, and challenge the enemy without the consent of their superiors, the entire army may face Ruin.

When the leader is weak and lazy, orders are not clear, the duties of officers and men are not distinctly outlined and everything is done in a slovenly manner, the entire army will be Disorganised.

If a general fails to know the enemy, pits a small force against a large force, matches weakness against strength, has no reliable vanguards, the result will be a complete Rout.

These principles regarding the causes of defeat and the responsibilities of the general should be clearly understood.

Advantageous terrain can help to win a battle, but the test of superior leadership lies in the ability to estimate and subdue enemy forces, to correctly assess the difficulties and dangers ahead.

He who applies these principles correctly will win and he who fails to do so will lose.

If he is sure of victory, a general should attack, even against his sovereign's orders.

If he is sure of defeat, a general should not engage in combat, even though his sovereign orders him to attack.

Neither because he wants to achieve fame when he orders an advance, nor because he fears personal disgrace when he orders a retreat, but always acting for the welfare of his soldiers and the benefit of his sovereign — such a general is the greatest treasure of the State.

A general who cares for his men as for his own children will be followed faithfully through the gravest dangers. He will have their support to the death.

However, if he is over-indulgent and does not know how to exercise authority, or if he is over-solicitous and cannot command obedience, his men will be like spoilt children, disobedient and disorderly, of no use at all.

A general who knows the strength of his own army but not the strength of the enemy has only a fifty per cent chance of victory.

If a general knows the strength of both the enemy army and his own, but is unaware of the difficulties of the terrain, his chances of victory are again halved.

The adept in warfare, once embarked on action, are able to cope with any kind of situation.

Thus, it may be said, "When one has a thorough knowledge of both the enemy and oneself, victory is assured. When one has a thorough knowledge of both heaven and earth, victory will be complete."

11

Positions

In warfare there are generally nine types of Positions, as follows:

(1) Dissentious

(2) Facile

(3) Critical

(4) Open

(5) Commanding

(6) Serious

(7) Fearful

(8) Beleaguered

(9) Desperate.

When a leader is fighting in his own territory, he is said to be in a Dissentious Position.

When he is fighting in enemy territory but has not penetrated far, he is said to be in a Facile Position.

When he is fighting for territory which would be advantageous for either side to possess, he is said to be in a Critical Position.

When he is fighting on ground which is equally accessible to both parties, he is in an Open Position.

When he is fighting in territory which occupies an important position in relation to several other states, so that control of that position would lead to control of the whole country, he is said to be in a Commanding Position.

When he has carried the fighting deep into hostile country and left in his rear many fortified enemy cities, he is in a Serious Position.

When he is fighting in mountainous forests, dangerous passes, marshy land or other difficult terrain, he is in a Fearful Position.

When he is fighting in country which is accessible only by narrow and tortuous paths which can be guarded easily by just a small force, or when he is hemmed in between narrow passes and strong enemy fortresses, he is said to be in a Beleaguered Position.

When he reaches the stage that all means of escape have been cut off and his only chance of survival lies in swift, hard fighting, he is in a Desperate Position.

In a Dissentious Position do not be the first to attack. Instead, try to inspire your men with a unity of purpose.

In a Facile Position keep your troops in close contact, but do not stop advancing.

In a Critical Position rush forward your reserve forces, but do not lay siege.

In a Open Position strengthen your defences rather than attempt a blockade.

In a Commanding Position use diplomacy to form strong ties with your allies.

In a Serious Position protect your supply routes but at the same time forage on the enemy.

In a Fearful Position, advance as swiftly as possible.

In a Beleaguered Position the way of retreat may be blocked and you must rely on stratagem.

In a Desperate Position fight to the death. There is no alternative.

A skilful general is able to prevent his enemy from

uniting, coordinating, reinforcing or rallying their forces.

When enemy forces are scattered, prevent them from reuniting. If they manage to regroup, try to create disorder.

Advance only when it is advantageous to do so. Otherwise, remain where you are.

To the question, "What can be done if a large and well organised army invades?" the answer is, "Try to seize whatever the enemy prize most and they can be made amenable."

Speed is essential in warfare. You must move faster than the enemy, appear where unexpected and attack when they are unprepared.

When fighting in hostile country, bear in mind the following principles:

The farther you penetrate, the more united your forces become and consequently, the more difficult to defeat.

If the land is fertile, proper foraging will secure adequate provisions for the whole army.

An army which is properly fed and spared unnecessary toil is able to conserve its energy and carry out orders swiftly and efficiently, thus surprising the enemy.

If an army is placed in a position from which there is no escape, the men will prefer death to disgrace.

If an army is placed in a position from which there is no escape without the strong risk of death, both officers and men will do their utmost.

Truly desperate men lose all fear of death; men conscious of the inevitable will stand firm; men deep in hostile country will fight stubbornly; men aware that they cannot afford to stop will fight all the harder.

Under such circumstances the soldiers are alert, willing, loyal and trustworthy, even when not under the close surveillance of their commanding officers. They will be free from superstitious fears and will not deviate from the path of duty, even if it leads to death. They will shun personal gain, even though no one is usually averse to wealth, and they will not be afraid to die, though life is precious. Upon being ordered into action men may moan and complain, but once they find themselves in a desperate situation they will be as courageous as the heroes of old (Zhu and Cao Gui).

The skilful in battle act with speed and coordination,

moving like the snake in Chang Mountain. If wounded in the head, it attacks with its tail; if wounded in the tail, it attacks with its head. If wounded in the middle, it attacks with both head and tail.

Can an army act with such speed and coordination? Can soldiers be made to cooperate with each other? The answer is "Yes". For example, the people of Wu State and Yue State had long been enemies. If some of them had been in the same boat in a storm, they would have cooperated for their common safety, just as the left and right hands come to help each other. However, when not confronted with a common danger, they did not trust each other, although they might ostentatiously disarm themselves, tethering war horses and burying chariots.

It is necessary to enforce strict discipline to make the army act in unison.

It is necessary to adapt to the terrain so that the army might have the greatest advantage in all circumstances.

A skilful leader is able to make his men obey him as easily and willingly as if he led them by the hand.

A general must remain calm and inscrutable, upright and strict. He should keep the army in ignorance of his plans, by deception if necessary, and frequently alter his tactics so that no one can be sure of his intentions. He should often change his plans and routes so that no one can anticipate his movements. The time to attack should be decided suddenly, as one might unexpectedly kick away the ladder by which one has ascended. Only after the army has penetrated deep into enemy territory may he reveal his plans. When he wants to make a determined drive, burning boats and breaking cooking utensils behind him, he should be like a shepherd driving his flock hither and thither without the "sheep" knowing their final destination.

He must lead when there are dangers ahead, and be victorious in spite of these dangers.

He must not fail to understand thoroughly the appropriate action to be taken in dealing with the nine different kinds of Situations discussed earlier in this chapter. He must comprehend and be able to employ the full range of offensive and defensive tactics and take into account the vagaries of human nature.

The deeper an army penetrates into enemy territory, the more united the invading force will be. If an invading army is stopped too near the boundary, dissension is likely to appear among the soldiers.

It is a proven fact that, if attacked, soldiers will defend themselves; if hard pressed they will fight; if desperate they will do anything.

Do not enter in to an alliance with any other State sovereign unless you fully know his plans.

Do not engage in battle before you are fully aware of the layout of the land — its mountains, passes, lakes, rivers, etc.

You need guides to take full advantage of the terrain.

If a sovereign fails to grasp these principles, he will not be a leader among the States.

If he wishes to be Emperor of many States, he must know how to avoid having to face the full force of an enemy more powerful than he is. If they are of an equal strength, he must be able to prevent the enemy from joining forces with their allies.

He should not fight against an alliance of enemy States, and he should not let any one State become unduly powerful in the Empire. He must try to win the confidence of those who can serve his purpose and also inspire fear in the hearts and minds of his enemies. In this way, he will be able to capture cities and overthrow enemy States.

If he does not reveal his plans beforehand, his soldiers

will not be sure what rewards or orders are in store, and they will follow him as one man.

Sometimes he must give orders without explaining his plans. He must show his men how to gain a certain objective without informing them of possible dangers.

If an army finds itself in a desperate position it will struggle to survive. When threatened with death men will fight hard for their lives. Only when they are beset with dangers will they do their utmost to turn defeat into victory.

In the conduct of warfare it is essential to be able to anticipate the enemy's plans.

When an army is able to make a concentrated attack, however distant the enemy, they can be defeated. It takes skill and ingenuity to succeed.

After very careful plans have been finalised, the soldiers should be isolated so that enemy spies and emissaries cannot get to them.

Every safeguard must be taken to keep secret the war plans which are deliberated in the ancestral temple, so that they may be executed successfully.

However, when there is any chance of learning enemy

secrets, it must be seized at once.

Secretly forestall the enemy by seizing first whatever they most prize.

Do not be inflexible in the conduct of a war. Vary your plans according to the conditions and the enemy. Let a decisive victory be your sole objective.

At the beginning, when enticing the enemy into combat, appear as shy as a young maiden. Then move as swiftly as a hare to catch the enemy while they are still unprepared.

12

Fire

Fighting with fire may take five forms:

(1) Burning men

(2) Burning stores

(3) Burning baggage trains

(4) Burning arsenals

(5) Destroying supply routes.

To wage war successfully with fire you need man-power and suitable weather as well as incendiary materials.

The dry season is the best time for warfare by fire and the best days to start a fire are when there is a strong wind caused by the four different positions of the moon.

To use any of the five forms of incendiarism to best advantage one should act as follows:

Attack as soon as the fire has taken a hold of the enemy camp.

If the fire fails to startle and confuse the enemy, hold back your attack.

When the fire has burned out, exercise discretion as to whether the enemy should be pursued.

If it is possible to start a fire outside, do not waste time trying to infiltrate the enemy camp to start a fire. The important thing is that the fire should be started at a favourable moment.

When attacking the enemy with fire, do not advance against the direction of the wind.

A wind which commences in the daytime will last, but one that starts blowing at night will soon stop.

One must not only know the five forms of incendiarism in warfare but also the appropriate measures in anticipation of them.

Those who attack with fire must have perspicacity, while those who attack with water must have strength.

By means of water you can cut off the enemy's supply route but you cannot rob them of their possessions.

After victory has been gained those who have rendered good service should be rewarded. Otherwise no one will have the incentive to do his utmost and the results would be calamitous.

It may be said that what a wise sovereign has planned a good general must execute.

Do not resort to war unless there is some definite advantage to be gained, and there is strong assurance of victory.

Do not fight unless the situation is so critical that there is no other alternative.

A sovereign should not start a war in a fit of anger; a general should not engage in battle out of spite.

The decision to wage war should be based on an objective consideration of possible gain. An angry man may be placated and his feelings changed; an aggrieved man may be calmed down; but a State, once destroyed, cannot be restored and a man killed cannot be brought back to life.

Therefore, a wise sovereign should hesitate before starting a war, while a good general should remain constantly alert in war. This will ensure peace for the State and the safety of the army.

13

Spies

It is expensive, both for the government and the people, to raise an army of one hundred thousand men and to campaign over a distance of one thousand *li*. Each day as much as thousands of *taels* of silver may be spent. The life of every class of people is disrupted and hordes are forced to toil on the road. As many as seven hundred thousand families may find it impossible to pursue their ordinary occupations.

A commander shows extreme lack of consideration for his men if he is too stingy to buy information from spies and thereby prolongs a war for years when victory might have been secured in a single day. Such a person cannot be a good leader or general, and is of no use to his sovereign.

Advance information about the enemy will enable a wise sovereign or a good general to win more victories and achieve greater success.

This information cannot be obtained by offering prayers to the gods and spirits, by inductive thinking or by deductive calculation; but only from men who have a thorough knowledge of enemy conditions.

Hence there is a great need of espionage and of spies, who may take 5 different forms:

(1)   Local Spies

(2)   Inside Spies

(3)   Converted Spies

(4)   Doomed Spies

(5)   Missionary Spies.

When all five kinds of spies are employed without the knowledge of the enemy, they can work wonders and be of invaluable assistance to the sovereign.

Local spies are recruited from among the inhabitants of the country, Inside Spies from among discontended officials of the enemy, and Converted Spies from the men whom the enemy have sent to do espionage work. Doomed Spies are those who purposely supply false information and are then denounced to the enemy by anonymous colleagues. Missionary Spies are those who are sent ostensibly on some mission but whose secret purpose is to bring back useful information.

In the whole army none should be more favourably regarded, liberally rewarded and clothed in secrecy than the spies.

Only the clever can be successful spies. Only the wise can pick the right men to do this work. Only with subtlety and ingenuity can the results of espionage be fully utilised.

An ingenious person can obtain secret information about anyone and anything.

If anyone reports the findings of a spy before they are made public, both the informant and the spy should be put to death.

In order to attack an army, storm a city or assassinate an individual, one must first send spies to obtain information regarding the commanding officers, their assistants, the servants and porters.

Every effort should be made to discover enemy spies who should then be well treated and bribed so that they may become Converted Spies, willing to work against their former masters.

With the help of Converted Spies one can recruit the services of Local Spies and Inside Spies. Furthermore, Converted Spies are in a position to identify and denounce Doomed Spies who have purposely passed on false information. Finally, it is through the assistance of Converted Spies that Missionary Spies are able to work according to plan.

The common goal of all five different kinds of spies is to obtain information about the enemy. The surest way to obtain this information is through Converted Spies, and so they should be treated with special generosity.

In ancient times the Yin (late Shang) Dynasty rose to power because of Yi Zhi, an official of the Xia Dynasty; and the Zhou Dynasty rose to power because of Lu Ya, an official of the Yin Dynasty.

It takes a wise leader to employ as spies men of the highest calibre only, with whose assistance success is sure. Spies are very important, for their information determines how a war should be conducted.